"WHEN A FRIEND DIES is excellent and will fill a great need.... Practical and powerful ideas."

– E.PAUL TORRANCE, GEORGIA
STUDIES OF CREATIVE BEHAVIOR

"This timely book furnishes teens with important information on understanding grief. Its unique format allows the reader to reflect on his or her experience with the death of a friend."

– SISTER TERESA M. MCINTIER,
PRESIDENT, GRIEF NETWORK COUNCIL

"This concise, easy to read book for teens who have experienced the trauma of losing a friend will help them begin to understand and deal with their own grief."

– PAT HENRY, PAST PRESIDENT,
NATIONAL PTA

"A valuable resource for school counselors."

– FREYDA SIEGEL, ED.M.,
MASSACHUSETTS COUNSELOR OF THE YEAR

When
A Friend
Dies

A Book for Teens About Grieving & Healing

Marilyn E. Gootman, Ed.D.
Edited by Pamela Espeland

free
Spirit
PUBLISHING

JUN '94

Gootman, Marilyn E., 1944–
        When a friend dies : a book for teens about grieving and healing/Marilyn E. Gootman
            p.   cm.
        Includes bibliographical references.
        ISBN 0-915793-66-0
        1. Grief in adolescence–Juvenile literature. 2. Bereavement in children–Juvenile literature. 3. Bereavement in adolescence–Juvenile literature. 4. Grief in children–Juvenile literature. 5. Teenagers and death–Juvenile literature. 6. Children and death–Juvenile literature.   (1. Death. 2. Grief.)   I. Title.
        BF724.3.G73G66   1994
        155.9'37'0835–dc20   93-37992
                                                        CIP
                                                        AC

10 9 8 7 6 5 4 3 2 1

Printed in the United States of America

Cover and book design by MacLean & Tuminelly

FREE SPIRIT PUBLISHING INC.
400 First Avenue North, Suite 616
Minneapolis, MN 55401
(612) 338-2068

Please note: Names have been changed throughout to protect the privacy of the students I spoke with in preparing this book.

W1

To my children, Elissa, Jennifer, and Michael

This book was inspired by my love and compassion for you and your friends. While I cannot protect you from losses, I hope I can help you through them.

Contents

Foreword

When a Friend Dies can help you to handle one of life's most difficult realities: the death of a friend. Marilyn Gootman understands what you are going through. Her advice and explanations are practical and perceptive. No matter how your friend died, no matter what you are feeling right now—guilty, angry, depressed, withdrawn, or all of these emotions—this book can help you to cope with your loss and pain.

Here you will find quotations from other teens whose friends have died. You will also find quotations from writers, philosophers, and other public figures whose wisdom and experience can guide you through your grief. If you share this book with your parents, teachers, and other caring adults, they will know more about how to give you the support you need during this hard time in your life.

In *When a Friend Dies*, you will find many ideas to talk over with others, and many ideas for grieving in healthy ways. You will notice that Marilyn Gootman does not judge you or tell you which feelings are "good" or "bad", "right" or "wrong." This may help you to let your feelings come without holding them back.

It may help you to talk about your feelings without thinking that you are "weird" or that you are the only person who feels the way you do. You are not alone. Other people who knew your friend are grieving, too.

Marilyn Gootman is an educator who works for the rights and needs of children and teenagers. *When a Friend Dies* is an important addition to the relatively short list of books written especially to help teenagers cope with and understand strong emotions. If you are grieving because your friend has died, you will find comfort here, as well as many ideas for helping yourself.

Deborah Prothrow-Stith, M.D.
Assistant Dean, Harvard School of Public Health
Author of *Deadly Consequences: How Violence is Destroying Our Teenage Population and a Plan to Begin Solving the Problem*

Introduction

"I just can't believe this happened to one of us."
— SETH

"I can't believe she is gone. She was so young and alive."
— ERICA

"It seems like any minute he should walk into the room. It doesn't seem like he is really gone."
— DAVID

Kids are not supposed to die. It's against all the rules of nature. It's not right. It's not fair. It shouldn't ever happen. But it does happen...and it's scary.

If your friend has died, this book is meant for you. I hope it will help you to understand what is happening to you and how you can help yourself heal. When my teenaged daughter's friend died a few years ago, I realized that most books written about death and dying don't speak directly *to* teenagers—they speak *about* them. This book speaks directly to you.

Sometimes I am the speaker. Sometimes the words are those of other teenagers whose friends have died.

Read this book all at once or in little pieces at a time. Think about the questions. Try the suggestions. Consider talking to a counselor or a therapist, if you think you need to; this book gives you ideas on where to start looking for help. Maybe you will want to read one or more of the other books listed at the end. You should do whatever works for *you*. You have had a terrible shock, and you need to take care of yourself. This book can be a part of taking care of yourself, if you want it to be.

Share this book with your parents and teachers. They need to know what you are going through, and this book may help them to understand. Especially if you sometimes have trouble putting your feelings into words, this book can speak for you.

Whatever you decide to do—about this book, about your grief, about anything in your life right now— I can promise you one thing: *You will heal with time.* You have probably heard this before. Maybe you don't believe it, but it's true. Not because I say so—because other teenagers say so. They have lived through, learned from, and grown by the horrible experience of having a friend die. You can, too.

How can I stand the pain?

Shock, terror, and disbelief may bombard your body and mind when a friend dies. Surely, it must be a mistake. How can it be—alive and breathing one minute and gone the next? The pain may seem unbearable. You may fear that your mind is on overload and you might go insane.

" When my friend died, the rest of the world kept going and no one knew what I was going through. No one could understand the pain I was feeling. I wanted the world to stop and I wanted to just scream out, 'Doesn't anyone realize that I am hurt, I am upset!' I wanted other people to stop their world and realize what I was going through. I kept looking at people and thinking, 'You don't have a care, and look at me, one of my friends just died.' **"**

— SELINA

" Things will never be the same. **"**

— JACOB

" I was sitting in class with her just yesterday. In two years when we graduate, she won't be there. **"**

— BETH

Don't panic! You won't always feel this bad. The pain will lessen as time goes on. After a while your sad feelings will become fewer and farther between and your happy feelings will return. Death gashes emotions just like a knife gashes skin. With time and care, both kinds of wounds heal. They leave scars, but they do heal.

Try to be gentle with yourself. When things start to get unbearably heavy, find a healthy, caring, loving way to distract yourself. Listen to music, write, draw, exercise....

What activities soothe you and keep your mind occupied when you feel overwhelmed? You don't have to do all of your grieving at once.

Why can't I feel anything?

You may be too stunned to feel anything. You may feel like you're living in a dream.

There is nothing wrong with you. Sometimes peoples' minds shut down when they feel overwhelmed. They shut out the reality of what has happened. This is your mind's way of protecting you from feeling overloaded with pain.

Give yourself some time to let your feelings surface. Then, when they're ready to come out, let them.

7

" *I cried hysterically, and then I went numb; kind of like I was watching myself from the outside.* **"**

— NICOLE

" *I can't feel anything. It doesn't feel real.* **"**

— DEVIN

How long will this last?

Dealing with death takes time—not just days, but weeks, months, and maybe even years.

You won't be in a perpetual state of gloom for the rest of your life. You won't always feel this bad. Grieving comes and goes. Sometimes you'll feel down and sometimes you won't.

Nature has a marvelous way of giving your mind and body a break from your hurt once in a while. You may feel sad, then be fine for a few months, then experience sadness and loss again at a later time. This cycle may repeat itself many times during your life.

There's no set timetable for grief. When you feel like grieving, then that is the right time for you. If you allow yourself to grieve, the hurt will get smaller and smaller as time goes on. The wound will slowly close up, leaving a healed scar.

"*The first day back to school was a bitter taste of reality, when you notice the absence. Even after the funeral I still in a way expected her to be there, like it was all a bad dream.*"

– SHANDA

"*I've come to realize that grief is something beyond one's control. Something else takes over like an involuntary muscle, working its way through the tragedy.*"

– AMY

Is it wrong to go to parties and have fun?

You have a right and a responsibility to enjoy life and get meaning out of it, even though your friend is gone. While you will have sad times, you are also entitled to laugh and have fun when you are in the mood. You do not need to feel guilty because you are having fun when your friend is not. Staying sad all the time is not going to help you or your friend.

What activities do you enjoy? Do you have any special hobbies? Is there a hobby you have always wanted to explore? Maybe now is the time to start.

How should I be acting?

There is no single right way to respond to death. Grief takes many different forms. Each person's grief is unique.

Crying

Some people sob and cry. Sadness wells up inside them and pours out.

Some people scream and wail. Maybe it helps them to let out their tension.

Some people just stay silent, sometimes crying by themselves, sometimes not. Just because people are quiet and don't talk about what happened doesn't mean that they aren't hurting. Sometimes people are so shocked or scared that they can't cry. Sometimes they are ashamed of admitting their feelings to others. Sometimes they cry inside.

Which is your way
of expressing your grief?

Sleeping

Some people go to bed and wake up at their usual times. They get a good night's sleep. Their minds are able to take a break from the pain.

Some people sleep much more than usual. Maybe sleep helps them to escape the pain, or maybe sleep comes because they are so tired from sadness and mourning.

Grieving takes a huge amount of mind and body energy. You can expect to feel tired.

Some people cannot sleep at all. Nightmares and scary thoughts keep jumping into their minds. They may not even be able to sit still. By keeping moving, they can push out painful thoughts that are more than they can stand.

"I can't sleep at night. I just keep going over the details in my mind, over and over."

— JOEL

Going without sleep can make you moodier and more sensitive. Here are some ideas to help you sleep:

- Read a funny book before bed.

- Listen to soothing music.

- Drink warm milk (it has a chemical in it that helps you relax).

- Watch a light, entertaining TV show or movie.

What other suggestions do you have? What works for you?

Eating

Some people eat like they usually do. Their bodies keep going like always. For them, eating is a habit that doesn't change.

Some people stop eating. The thought of food turns them off. They may even forget to eat. Sometimes their insides are so tied up in knots that it hurts to eat. Some may vomit.

Some people cannot stop eating. Food, especially sweets, can be comforting at times like these.

Have your eating patterns changed? Think about what you are eating. Try to choose foods that are good for you. Eating sweets may make you feel better for a short time, but the "sugar crash" that follows will make you feel worse.

Will I be changed?

As time goes on, some people begin to act like they used to. They do not seem to be changed by the experience of having a friend die. They may feel changed on the inside but don't show it on the outside.

Some people become silly and giddy. They may joke and fool around a lot because of the tension they feel. They hurt, even if it doesn't look that way.

Some people may become quiet and very sad. They may not want to be cheered up, but they may want to talk.

Do you think you

have changed? If so, how?

Do you think people are treating

you differently now? How does

that make you feel?

What is "normal"?

All these different ways of reacting to the death of a friend are "normal." Don't judge yourself or others by the way you act or the way they act. Pain is pain, no matter how it looks on the outside. Don't waste your time comparing one person's reactions to another's, or one person's pain to another's. You all hurt, and you all have the right to express it in your own special ways.

Before your friend died, you may have thought that all people grieve by crying. Now you know that this isn't true for everyone. Sometimes you can clearly see another person's sadness and hurt. Sometimes you can't see them at all. And sometimes people camouflage their true feelings. They may act giddy or boisterous even though they are hurting inside.

What if I hardly knew the person?

You don't have to be a person's best friend to feel the pain of grief when he or she dies. Even if you just knew about the person, you may feel pain.

You may be reminded of other losses you experienced earlier in your life. You may be frightened by the realization that if this person died, you could die, too. You may have liked or admired the person even though you didn't know him or her well.

You have the right to your pain. Don't compare it to the pain of someone else who knew the person better. Pain is pain.

How can I handle my feelings?

Many thoughts pass through people's minds when they are grieving. These thoughts often trigger strong feelings. Understanding these feelings will help you heal.

"If only..."

"If only I had done...."

"If only I had said...."

"If only...."

These are thoughts that torment many people when someone dies. The truth is that awful things happen and often nobody can stop them.

Sometimes people are powerless, but to admit that you are powerless can be very scary. Feeling guilty is one way to avoid feeling powerless. That is why you may find yourself thinking, "If only...."

"I regretted not begging my sister to come to college with me...I felt she didn't know how much I really did care about her. If only she had known, she might not have killed herself."

— FELICIA

"If only she hadn't gone to pick up her boyfriend at the airport."

— RUTH

Death is scary. It makes us feel so powerless. If you feel guilty because you think you should have done something to stop your friend's death, or that you might have done something to cause it, this may be your mind's way of helping you not to feel so powerless. But you are not guilty. It is not fair to expect yourself to stop another person's death.

If your friend died in an accident or from an illness, then your "if only's" are your mind's way of helping you feel some control in your life at a very out-of-control time. If your friend died by suicide, it was your friend's decision, not yours. You are not responsible for that decision. You could not control your friend's thoughts or actions any more than someone else can control yours.

Be fair to yourself. Be kind to yourself. It is very unlikely that you could have done anything to stop your friend's death.

"I wish..."

"I wish I had been nicer to my friend..."

"I wish we hadn't had that argument..."

"I wish I could take back what I said..."

This is another way guilt shows its ugly face. The truth is that arguments, fights, and anger are all part of normal living and feeling. Nobody is perfect, not even the person who died. Life would be very boring if we all tiptoed around each other, afraid to disagree or to be angry because we thought another person might die soon. What went on before has nothing to do with your friend's death.

"I wish I had listened to him. I should have done something."

— TERRELL

Sometimes people are afraid to say anything bad about someone who has died. They turn the dead person into a saint. Every person in this world has strong points and weak points, even those who have died. Loving someone means being honest and accepting the whole person, both the good and the bad, even if the person is dead.

"When I was in sixth grade my best friend was killed in a car accident....The next day at school I can remember how our class acted. No one was allowed to touch her desk—a rule someone in our class made. It was almost like a shrine...."

– CARLA

"My mind is frozen.
I can't think."

The shock of a sudden death makes some people feel as if their minds are frozen. This may be nature's way of protecting your mind so that everything can sink in slowly and you won't be overwhelmed. If you talk to others and share your sadness, your mind will slowly begin to defrost and you will start to adjust to your loss.

"I'm just numb. I can't study or be with friends or do anything."

— ENRICO

Sometimes it may seem easier to stay frozen and just deny that you are even bothered by what happened. Denying something will not make it go away. Denying your feelings will only keep your hurts inside so they cannot come out and be healed. If a friend dies, it has to be hard on you. Try to admit it to yourself, and talk to someone understanding.

"Why did you let it happen?"

Red-hot anger often comes out after someone has died. You may want to blame someone for your friend's death—another person, your friend's parents, a boyfriend or girlfriend, or God. You might even be angry at your friend for dying—for being careless, for getting sick, for not wearing a seat belt, for drinking, for taking his or her own life, or just for leaving you.

> "First my grandfather died, and then a month later my best friend was accidentally killed. What does God have against me?"
>
> — PATRICK

> "It's not fair! She didn't deserve to die."
>
> — KEISHA

You have a right to be angry. It is not fair that your friend has died—not for your friend, and not for you. Go ahead and feel angry. But be careful not to turn your anger onto yourself or others. Be sure to get your anger out in a way that will not hurt anyone.

Run, work out, or go to a place where you can yell at the top of your lungs. Try to think of constructive ways to use the energy from your anger. Build something. Make something. Do whatever you can to release some of your anger. Most important, talk about it.

Or you can try to use your anger to make this world a better place. Some suggestions:

- Form a Students Against Driving Drunk chapter at your school. (See page 95 for more information.)

- Start a seat belt campaign.

- Start a hotline for teenagers.

- Do whatever else makes sense to you.

What would help you

to release your anger

and calm down?

"How could you leave me?"

It is normal to feel lonely and left behind after a friend dies. The death has ripped a hole in your life. Your friend is gone, and now it seems as if you must work it out alone.

But you are not alone. Reach out to other people, including those you may not have been friendly with in the past. Try to share your pain. If they knew your friend, they may be suffering, too. By sharing your pain, you will all begin to heal.

"Why did my friend have to die? She was so pretty and smart and nice. Sometimes I feel like it should've been me that died instead."

— PENNY

Talk to your parents, if you can. If you can't, there are many other adults who can listen—counselors, teachers, other relatives, religious or spiritual leaders. If you know the parents of the person who died, try talking to them. They may appreciate it more than you will ever know.

*You may feel
alone and left behind, but you
are not alone. You have a whole
community around you
that shares your loss.*

"When my best friend was killed, my mom went to the viewing and told me how she looked and I did not want to go. I wanted to remember her alive and beautiful. I did go to the funeral. This was a way for me to realize it was real. I felt like I was there but not really. My mind did not want to accept it. My family did a lot to help me by talking to me."

— NICK

Is there someone you would feel comfortable talking to? Maybe a parent. Maybe a teacher. Or maybe another person your age who also knew your friend who died.

Try to approach him or her and begin to chat about anything—the weather, sports, school, a popular movie.... Don't feel as if you have to start talking about your friend's death right away. Let the conversation come around to it. The other person may want to talk about it as much as you.

"I'm afraid to get close to someone else. What if that person dies, too?"

The pain of losing a friend can be excruciating. It makes sense to want to avoid ever feeling such pain again. But isolating yourself from other people because you're afraid of losing them will only make your pain worse by increasing your loneliness.

It is unlikely that another friend will die. Of course, there is no guarantee. But there *is* a guarantee that reaching out to friends can lessen your pain and help you through this difficult time.

*Needing a friend
at this time is a tribute to
your friend who died. After all,
your friend helped you to realize
the importance of friendship.*

"If I get close to other people, won't I betray my friend who died?"

Some people think that if they make new friends they are not being loyal to the friend who died. They go out of their way to avoid new friendships. This doesn't help you, and it doesn't help your friend who died. You can remain loyal to your friend and still reach out to others. Your friend who died will always remain in your heart and in your mind.

"My best friend was shot and killed. We were best friends since I was four years old—almost ten years. Now I feel angry all the time. I even got mad at a friend who came over to see me. It's like I don't want a friend anymore."

— DARYL

"Some of my friends have changed. I feel like I have lost them, too."

People react in different ways when someone dies. Some may need to break away from painful reminders of the friend they have lost. These "reminders" might include friends they shared in common. Others may be so very sad that they just don't seem the same. Either way, this may feel like another loss to you. As you open up and talk to people, you may find yourself making new friends and also slowly returning to your old friends.

"We don't feel close like a group anymore. The guys won't come over and be with us."

— MARISA

Look around.

Do you see anybody who might

be an interesting friend?

"I feel like I am going crazy."

Sometimes you may feel like you will go out of your mind thinking about what happened. The fact that death is so final is frightening not just for you but for all of us. Close your mind down for a while if you have to. Blank out the scary thoughts to give your mind a rest.

"After my friend died, I began to worry that my parents would die or that I might die."

— CARLOS

"Who will it be next time?"

— MAX

Sometimes it may be hard to stop thinking about your friend and what happened. Bad thoughts may come into your mind even when you're enjoying yourself. This happens to many people. Sometimes people feel guilty about having fun. They let bad thoughts into their minds on purpose so they will not enjoy themselves.

You have a right and a responsibility to live your life and enjoy it. You cannot help your friend by holding yourself back from living your life to the fullest.

If you feel overwhelmed, take a break. Think of a way to escape from your thoughts and feelings. Call a friend, go for a walk, watch a movie, take deep breaths. What works for you?

"All of a sudden it hits me and I get sad."

Sometimes you may find that certain situations— hearing a certain song on the radio, being in a certain place, a change in the weather, words, a smell—remind you of your friend. They may even remind you of when and how your friend died. You may become very sad, anxious, even panicky. This happens to so many people who have lost someone in a sudden, shocking way that it has been given a special name: *post-traumatic stress.*

Post-traumatic stress can take many forms: nightmares, pictures in your mind of your friend's death, fear that someone else close to you will die, painful sadness. You can experience post-traumatic stress whenever something reminds you of when and how your friend died.

Try to notice when this happens to you. Tell yourself that it is a normal reaction. Be gentle with yourself.

You are not crazy! Millions of other people share your reaction. Knowing what it is about can help you deal with it.

"In the car on the way to the funeral my mind became flooded with memories. Slowly at first the scenes appeared in my mind's eye and then built up to frantic speeds. The whole time I sat and stared straight through the windshield while my brain sifted, sorted, filed, and preserved."

– ANNA

"I'd better enjoy myself as much as I can now, because who knows what tomorrow may bring?"

Yes, you should enjoy your life every day. You can do this by living a full life and doing things you enjoy that make you feel worthwhile—things that give your life meaning. But it is foolish and reckless to do self-destructive things—such as drinking, taking drugs, or driving too fast—because you figure you should enjoy yourself now, while you have the chance. Why run the risk of destroying your life? If you live a long life, and you probably will, won't this attitude hurt you in the long run?

"After my friend died, all I could think was, 'Be young, stay young, raise hell while young.'"

– ROY

Some people think that when a friend dies, this reduces the chances that something bad will happen to them. It's as if one death in a group of friends somehow "protects" the other friends from harm. Statistically, your chances of dying are not any lower—or any higher—now than they were before your friend died. That is why you should still take good care of yourself. Risky behaviors are still risky behaviors.

How many ways
can you have fun without
hurting or endangering
yourself or others?

"My parents are hovering over me and smothering me."

Most parents want to protect their children from hurt, and what is more hurtful than the death of a friend? You're right about feeling that they can't and shouldn't protect you from this hurt. You want to believe that you can handle it. When your parents hover, this makes you think that you *can't* handle it.

You have a right to your own space if you need it. You shouldn't feel guilty about wanting your parents to back off. But tell them kindly, not harshly or hurtfully. Remember that your friend's death has scared them, too. Of course they want to hold you close; the idea that someone could lose a child has become all too real for them. They may be afraid of losing *you*.

Here are some things you may want to tell your parents:

- "I love you, and I know you love me."

- "I know you are worried about me because of what has happened."

- "I need to deal with this. Please don't try to protect me."

- "Please don't tell me how to feel."

- "When I talk to you about my feelings, I'd appreciate it if you just listened."

- "Sometimes I may not want to talk to you. I may want to talk to my friends instead. They are going through the same thing I'm going through. We understand each other."

- "Sometimes I may want to talk to another adult—a teacher, counselor, or minister. This doesn't mean that I'm rejecting you—just that I want to talk to someone who isn't so close to me."

On page 103, you'll find a brief list of suggested readings—books that can help you better understand what you're going through and why. You may want to share this list with your parents. Maybe they will want to read some of the books, too.

How can I deal with my grief?

Healing any wound, in the body or the mind, takes time. Allow yourself that time. You are entitled to it. Give yourself permission to grieve. Allow yourself to grieve when and where you need to. Share your feelings. Write about them. Draw them. Talk to others about your feelings.

Even though you may feel sad when you talk about your friend, talking will help your pain get smaller. Not talking won't make your pain go away. In fact, it may make it stronger. As you force your pain to stay inside, it pushes against you, trying to get out. That's why it's so important to find someone—a friend or an adult—to talk to. Sharing your feelings with others is a healthy way to release some of your pain.

Sometimes when people don't take time to grieve, they become very angry. Often they explode at other people and situations that have nothing to do with the death. Try to think of your emotions inside you as steam inside a pipe. Just as a steam valve slowly releases steam so the pipe won't burst, you can set aside time to slowly grieve so your emotions won't spill out unpredictably and harmfully.

If you set aside time to grieve, you will eventually be able to block out your grief at other times. This may be particularly helpful when you really need to concentrate and cannot be distracted, such as during a test. Later, when you are ready, you can come back to your grief.

Remember to live your life to the fullest. Try to think of something positive you learned from your friend, something funny that happened when you were together, or a pleasant time you shared. Know that a part of your friend will always remain with you.

"When looking back on your lost loved one, try to picture them at their healthiest and happiest."

— THERESA

What are your fondest memories

of your friend?

How can I help myself heal?

Share, talk with others, write, draw, listen to music, write music, cuddle with a pet or a stuffed animal, or plant a tree in memory of your friend. Visit your friend's parents. It might be hard to see them, but you can help each other.

Many people find that reaching out to others, doing good deeds, and making the world a better place can help them to heal from the death of a friend.

*How could
you translate your
pain into positive actions that
would be a tribute to your friend?*

*What would be a way to keep your
friend's memory alive—a
meaningful memorial to
your friend?*

What if I can't handle my grief on my own?

Many people who have experienced a great loss find it helpful to speak to someone who has been specially trained to guide people through grieving. Speaking to a counselor or therapist (psychologist, psychiatrist, social worker) when you have been hurt by death is no different from going to a medical doctor when you have a deep cut. Both kinds of professionals are trained to help people heal.

Your first visit to a counselor or therapist may be a bit scary and embarrassing. But if the person is in tune with your hurt—if he or she is willing to listen to you and understand your point of view—you will soon feel relieved to have this person to talk to.

If you need to speak to a counselor or a therapist after a friend has died, you are not "sick." You have been injured by events beyond your control, and you are getting help for your injury. It's that simple.

What if my friends start acting strange?

Many people who have suffered a sudden, shocking loss could be helped by talking with a counselor or a therapist. In particular, teenagers who are behaving in unusual ways could probably use some guidance. Keep an eye out for friends who...

...drink and take drugs to numb their pain

...stop eating, or eat very little

...eat a lot and force themselves to vomit

...suddenly start doing very poorly in school

...talk about wanting to give up and die.

Have you noticed any of these behaviors in a friend? If so, speak to a responsible, caring adult—the school counselor, a teacher, your friend's parent, your own parent, a minister, priest, or rabbi. Let that person find help for your friend.

No, you are not betraying your friend. You are being a true, loving friend. The right thing to do—the most caring thing to do—is to tell a responsible, caring adult. You can't solve your friend's problems on your own. That would be an unfair burden for you to carry all by yourself.

Read the list of behaviors on page 83 again. Have you noticed any of them in yourself? If so, please get the help you need and deserve.

What adult

   can you approach

      to discuss your friend...or yourself?

         Who would be a calm listener?

         Who would know where to steer

            you to get the help you need?

How can I find a counselor or a therapist?

• If possible, get a personal referral.

Is there someone you know who goes to a counselor or a therapist? If you both feel comfortable talking about it, ask for the name of the counselor or therapist. Ask the person's opinion of the counselor or therapist. Has he or she been helped by the experience?

If you don't know someone who is seeing a counselor or a therapist, ask another person you trust for some suggestions. Good possibilities might include your school counselor, your school psychologist, a teacher, your doctor, or your clergy person.

- If you can't get a personal referral, see about resources in your community.

Check the phone book or call Information to find out the names and numbers of the local mental health clinic, pastoral counseling center, family service agency, hospital, or a university or college counseling psychology department. These places go by different titles in different towns, but the operator should be able to help you figure out the correct title.

You can call any of these places and ask for a referral. Many of them help people on a sliding scale fee basis, which means that you pay only what you can afford. You can also contact the national organizations listed on pages 92–93 of this book. They will give you the names of counselors or therapists who belong to their organizations and who live in your area.

- Look in the Yellow Pages under "therapists,"
  "social workers," "counselors," "psychologists,"
  "psychiatrists," or "psychotherapy."

Getting a name out of the phone book is a bit risky.
Just because someone has a title doesn't guarantee
that he or she is the right person for you to see and
talk to. At the very least, you should try to find
someone who specializes in working with teenagers
and/or grief work.

- Instead of finding an individual counselor or therapist, consider joining a support group.

A support group is a group of people who share problems similar to yours. They meet regularly with a counselor or a therapist. Support groups can be very effective, especially for people who are grieving. Knowing that others are experiencing thoughts and reactions like yours, and being with people who reach out and support each other, can help you heal.

Sometimes support groups are available in schools, especially when a student has died. If your school doesn't offer support groups, check with a counselor or therapist, social worker, or mental health agency. Someone will help you to find a group that is right for you.

How can I tell if a counselor or therapist can help me?

You have many choices when it comes to seeking help. School counselors, psychologists, psychiatrists, social workers, psychiatric nurses, certified mental health workers, and pastoral counselors (clergy) are all qualified to provide therapy. But only you can decide whether someone is qualified to be *your* counselor or therapist. Here are some questions to ask yourself about someone you are considering:

- Does he or she seem to understand my feelings?

- Has he or she experienced the death of a friend? (This isn't essential, but it often helps.)

- Can he or she listen without being judgmental?

- Am I comfortable being honest with him or her?

- Does he or she accept me in a way that helps me to accept myself?

Remember: Counseling or therapy is meant to ease your pain. Only you can tell whether it is working for you. If one person doesn't seem to be helping, try someone else. Keep trying until you find someone who is right for you.

National organizations to contact for referrals

The American Psychiatric Association
1400 K Street, NW
Washington, DC 20005
Telephone: (202) 682-6000

You can ask for the phone number of the district branch in your state. The district branch will give you the names and phone numbers of some psychiatrists in your area. Psychiatrists are medical doctors who are trained to help people deal with emotional problems.

The American Psychological Association
750 First Street, NE
Washington, DC 20002-4242
Telephone: (202) 336-5700

Ask to be connected to the Public Affairs office. They will give you the phone number of your local state psychological association. When you call that number, someone there will give you further guidance in finding a psychologist. Psychologists usually have received a doctoral degree from a university.

The National Association of Social Workers
750 First Street, NE
Suite 700
Washington, DC 20002
Telephone: (202) 408-8600

Ask for the Clinical Register Office. They will give you a list of registered clinical social workers in your area. Clinical social workers have received advanced education and training to help people deal with emotional problems.

Organizations for specific causes

American Association of Suicidology (AAS)
2459 South Ash Street
Denver, CO 80222
Telephone: (303) 692-0985

AAS can let you know if there is a support group in your area for "suicide survivors"—people who know someone who committed suicide. They also have a list of crisis centers around the country and a Survivors of Suicide Resource List which contains suggestions of books, films, and pamphlets that might be helpful to suicide survivors.

The Dougy Center
3909 SE 52nd Avenue
PO Box 86852
Portland, OR 97286
Telephone: (503) 775-5683

The Dougy Center offers support groups for grieving children and young people ages 3–19, with special groups for teenagers. They also offer training and intervention services at sites around the country. Contact them to learn about groups in your area.

National Self-Help Clearinghouse
25 West 43rd Street
Room 620
New York, NY 10036
Telephone: (212) 642-2944

The clearinghouse can give you information about self-help groups. If you send them a self-addressed, stamped envelope, they will send you information about their services and publications.

Students Against Driving Drunk (SADD)
PO Box 800
Marlboro, MA, 01752
Telephone: (508) 481-3568

SADD can provide you with information about how to start a SADD (Students Against Driving Drunk) chapter in your school.

A promise to you... and some words that may help you to heal

I wish that this had never happened to you and your friend, but it did. There is nothing you can do to change what has happened, but there is much you can do to help yourself. I have gone through what you are going through now. I know people your age whose friends have died. I can make this promise: You will grow from this tragedy. You will learn more about yourself and others. You will become more sensitive. Your view of the world will change.

No one would ever choose to grow because of the death of a friend. But now that it has happened to you, what can you do to make meaning out of your experience? Think about that in the weeks, months, and years ahead. You will find a way.

Meanwhile, you may take some comfort in the words of others who have spoken or written about death. Read the quotations on the next few pages. If there is one that is especially inspiring or helpful to you, write it down on a piece of paper and carry it in your wallet or calendar. Or create your own quotation. Share your words with a friend who is also grieving. Help each other.

"No willpower could prevent someone's dying."
— ANNIE DILLARD

"Whenever tragedy strikes and people ask, 'Why did this have to happen to me?' I always want to say to them, 'Why not you? Are you so much different from the rest of the human race?'"
— WINNIE JOHNSON

"Death is the sound of distant thunder at a picnic."
—W.H. AUDEN

"Life is what we make it, always has been, always will be."
— GRANDMA MOSES

" *We are healed of a suffering only by experiencing it to the full.* **"**

                             – MARCEL PROUST

" *Since every death diminishes us a little, we grieve— not so much for the death as for ourselves.* **"**

                             – LYNN CAINE

" *Between grief and nothing I will take grief.* **"**

                             – WILLIAM FAULKNER

" *The hundreds of people around you cannot console you for the loss of the one.* **"**

                             – MARIA AUGUSTA TRAPP

"Grief melts away
Like snow in May
As if there were no such cold thing. "
— GEORGE HERBERT

"One must go through periods of numbness that are
harder to bear than grief. "
— ANNE MORROW LINDBERGH

"I still miss those I loved who are no longer with me
but I find I am grateful for having loved them. The
gratitude has finally conquered the loss. "
— RITA MAE BROWN

"Sorrow was like the wind. It came in gusts. "
— MARJORIE KINNAN RAWLINGS

"*All sorrows can be borne if you put them into a story or tell a story about them.*"

— Isak Dinesen

"*Life was meant to be lived, and curiosity must be kept alive. One must never, for whatever reason, turn his back on life.*"

— Eleanor Roosevelt

"*Death is not the enemy; living in constant fear of it is.*"

—Norman Cousins

"*You don't get to choose how you're going to die. Or when. You can only decide how you're going to live. Now.*"

— Joan Baez

Suggested readings

Gordon, Sol. *When Living Hurts.* (New York: Dell, 1989.)

Kübler-Ross, Elisabeth. *On Death and Dying.* (New York: Macmillan, 1993.)

Kushner, Harold. *When Bad Things Happen to Good People.* (New Jersey: Outlet Book Co., 1990.)

Notes

Notes

About the author

Marilyn E. Gootman, Ed. D., is a nationally recognized speaker and writer who focuses on the rights and needs of children. She conducts workshops for students, teachers, parents, social workers, counselors, and foster parents on topics ranging from grief to discipline. Her media appearances include CNN, CBS News, "Sonya Friedman Live," and "Nightwatch." Hundreds of thousands of copies of her discipline brochure for parents, "Would You Like to Wear the Red or Blue Socks?," have been distributed by the National Committee for the Prevention of Child Abuse. Dr. Gootman is a member of the faculty of the College of Education at the University of Georgia in Athens, Georgia. She and her husband, Elliot, have three children: Elissa, Jennifer, and Michael. If you would like more information about Dr. Gootman's workshops, please contact her c/o Free Spirit Publishing, 400 First Avenue North, Suite 616, Minneapolis, MN 55401.

**For a free copy of our
SELF–HELP FOR KIDS®
catalog, write or call:**

Free Spirit Publishing
400 First Avenue North, Suite 616
Minneapolis, MN 55401

**1–800–735–7323
612–338–2068**